Utterly LOST IN TRANSLATION

Do you have a suggestion for a future volume?
I'd love to hear from you via my website:
www.theimportanceofbeingtrivial.com.

Utterly LOST IN TRANSLATION

EVEN MORE MISADVENTURES IN ENGLISH ABROAD

CHARLIE CROKER

ILLUSTRATED BY ANDREW PINDER

First published by Metro Publishing,
an imprint of
John Blake Publishing Limited
3 Bramber Court, 2 Bramber Road
London W14 9PB

www.johnblakebooks.com

www.facebook.com/johnblakebooks
twitter.com/jblakebooks

First published in hardback in 2015

ISBN: 978-1-78418-385-1

British Library Cataloguing-in-Publication Data:

A catalogue record for this book is available from the British Library.

Design by www.envydesign.co.uk

Printed in Great Britain by CPI Group (UK) Ltd

3 5 7 9 10 8 6 4 2

Papers used by John Blake Publishing are natural, recyclable products made from wood grown in sustainable forests. The manufacturing processes conform to the environmental regulations of the country of origin.

Contents

Acknowledgements

Many thanks to all the readers who supplied examples for this book. Lack of space prevents me from listing you all, but special mentions must go to Chiara Bertoglio, Rosemary Dennehy, Brian Gould, Freddie Greenwood, Rebekah Gregoriades, Heinz Kozu, John O'Shea, Hella Trawny and John Tydeman. Once again Rob Heeley's global tours have garnered whole suitcases of material. Thanks also to Alexander Chancellor and Jeremy Clarke, for dispatches from Italy and India respectively.

I'm indebted as ever to Special Agent Charlie Viney. And working on this book has brought me the pleasure not just of Toby Buchan's impeccable editorship but also his anecdotes and trivia about everything from George III to London bank robberies. I'm hugely grateful to him and everybody at John Blake.

CHARLIE CROKER

Introduction

Once more unto the breach, dear friends! The breach of contract between English and the people speaking it, that is. Yes, nearly a decade after *Lost in Translation* first collected language howlers from across the globe, it's time to update the search for the world's most amusing errors. It's time to get *utterly* lost in translation.

All the old fertile hunting grounds are here, of course – hotels, restaurants, instruction leaflets and the like. But since that first book stuck its head above the verbal parapet, new sources of delight have appeared. The computer-generated TV subtitle, for instance. In the mid-noughties this technology was in its infancy. Now it has improved so much that it's a fixture of modern media life. Most of the time it works just fine. Once in a while, however, the oh-so-clever software gets things that little bit wrong. And so it is that when the newsreader mentions the Archbishop of Canterbury, the screen displays it as 'the arch bitch of Canterbury'. Instead of reporting 'five hundred badgers are set to be killed', the screen announces 'five hundred actors are set to be killed'.

Another burgeoning source of amusement is the spam email. It's astonishing, given the cleverness with which techno-shysters make a message look as though it really has come from your bank, reproducing email addresses and graphics with pixel-perfect accuracy, that they pay so little attention to the words in the emails themselves. The comically inept English gives the game away even before the end of the first sentence. Would the real NatWest send you a message advising that 'protective measures is been applied to satisfy out striving costumer needs'?

So, enjoy these latest morsels from the front line of the war on accuracy. But remember, as ever, that for all the amusement we Brits get from foreigners' efforts with English, at least they *make* an effort. We swan around the planet, arrogantly refusing to attempt a single syllable of their languages. One of my informants reports she heard a British person in France, when confronted with a sign saying 'Hotel Restaurant', respond with: 'How nice – they've written it in English, just for us.'

Getting there... or not

They say that the journey of a thousand miles begins with a single step. The trouble is, it often ends with a single badly translated notice...

SIGN ON CABIN DOOR, SLEEPER TRAIN, VENICE TO PARIS:

This compartiment is equipe of a detector of fire. In the event of declenchement of audible alarm, evacuer the compartiment without precipitatation and come into contact with the crew.

SIGN, PORT OF VENICE:

ALLOWED ACCESS
ONLY TO HIM
AUTHORIZED.

IN TERMS AND CONDITIONS OF TURKISH AIRLINES TICKET:

After departure ticket is non-refundable in case of refund.

STANSTED AIRPORT, UK:

Help us to reduce queues. Please stand in line.

SIGN ON REAR OF TRUCK, NEW DELHI, INDIA:

Don't fast.

AIRPORT, CHINA:

This is a civilized airport.

HOTEL GUEST INFORMATION BOOKLET, THAILAND:

If you are thinking of hiring a car please drive carefully as all Thai drivers have a death wish.

TRAIN, ITALY:

Do not damage or dirty the railways carriages.

Passengers disregarding the above-mentioned regulations must bear the resulting consequences.

SIGN FOR WHEELCHAIR-ACCESSIBLE ROAD, CHINA:

Traffic lan for defromed man.

METRO STATION, SHANGHAI, CHINA:

If you are stolen, call the police at once.

ROAD SIGN, INDIA:

GO SLOW – accident porn area.

INDIAN TAXI DRIVER TO BRITISH MALE PASSENGER:

'In Rajasthan, if you have strong penis you can get a lot of lady, sir.'

SIGN IN FRONT OF RESTAURANT, MEXICO CITY, MEXICO:

Valet Porking.

ON BACK OF LORRY, MANIPUR STATE, INDIA:

In trust we God.

GO SLOW
accident
porn area

ON BACK OF TAXI, THAILAND:

How is my driving? How is my attitude? If you think I should be change my attitude please contact us.

ROAD SIGN AT EXIT FROM VILLAGE, ALGERIA:

Au Revoir
Goodbye
Bon route
Good road.

ON BACK OF RICKSHAW, INDIA:

Snake poison is better than Lady Smile.

NOTICE AT BANGALORE CANTONMENT TRAIN STATION, INDIA, EARLY 1980s:

Ticketless traveller heavy penalty awaits.

NOTICE OVER WASHBASIN IN TRAIN TOILET, YUGOSLAVIA, 1957:

For to obtain of water reverse handle indifferently to left and right.

NOTICE IN SMALL AIRCRAFT, JAPAN:

Such as scissors, knives, cutlery, bringing in an aircraft shall be deemed to be the other weapon, the law.

Are prohibited.

In addition, hazardous substances such as flammable fire brought into the aircraft, and even entrusted the handling of baggage.

Not.
If you are in possession of restricted items carry, or will put us in the baggage, leave the security checkpoint.

We ask you at the disposal.

If you are in possession of dangerous goods, we ask you to waste as the security checkpoint at the start.

FAQ SECTION FROM THE SAME AIRLINE'S WEBSITE:

Q: When buying airline tickets on credit cards can I pay?
A: Buy our ticket desk in cash has become only your credit card will not be accepted.
In addition, the airport terminal, the bank ATM, etc. Please note no.

Q: What do I how long before the flight attendant?
A: Departure 30 minutes ago. Please come by.
Please visit us have the time to spare.

Q: If I heard that bad weather might be cancelled?
A: Departure, if the Company falls below the standard operation of the destination and weather conditions may be canceled. And may be operated again after waiting for the recovery of the weather.

Q: Is there a bathroom on the plane?
A: The cabin has no toilet facilities. Please complete your in terminal before boarding.

OUT-OF-ORDER TICKET MACHINE, GARE DU NORD, PARIS, FRANCE:

Temporarily inalienable terminal. Please excuse us for the caused embarrassment.

SIGN IN CAR PARK, AQUARIUM, AUSTRALIA:

Beware Children Drive Slowly.

INSTRUCTIONS FOR REAR-VIEW MONITOR, TOYOTA PRIUS, 2010:

As it becomes hard to see if a stain or a drop sticks, clean the camera lens without hurting it.

SIGN IN AIRPORT CAR PARK, CHINA:

Please confirm your car is licked.

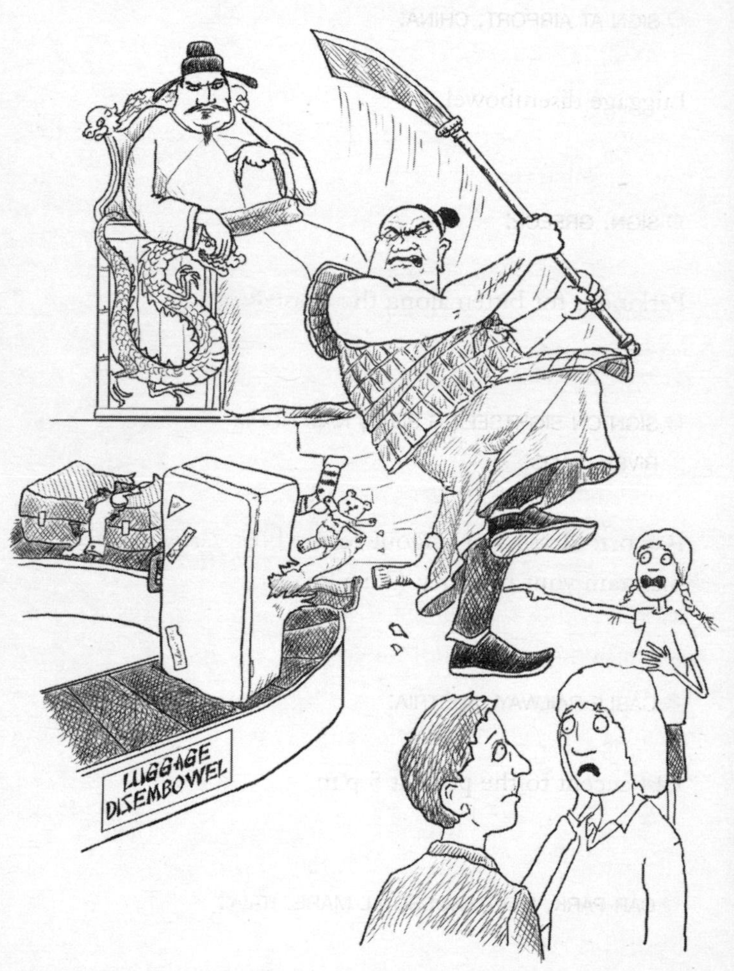
LUGGAGE
DISEMBOWEL

SIGN AT AIRPORT, CHINA:

Luggage disembowel.

SIGN, GREECE:

Parking is for bitten along the coastal road.

SIGN ON SIGHTSEEING BOAT, NAM NGUM RIVER, LAOS:

Report: Please you singout to the boat can you checking maintain your property. (Thank you).

CABLE RAILWAY, AUSTRIA:

Last accent to the peak at 5 p.m.

CAR PARK, MONTEROSSO AL MARE, ITALY:

1) It is paid only when the vehicle witdrawes him
2) To preserve the token not to lose

3) The automatic box is paid to is found next to the door of the staircases to the plain earth
4) Recommend him effected the paiment 10 minutes of time are had only for going out of the parking lot.

SIGN ON BOAT, GREECE:

Boarding this vessel is deemed valid consent to inspect persons artifacts and effect. Refusal to inspect will result in boarding denied & reporting to authorities.

CAR FERRY, GREECE:

Passengers please not to stand on the dock since dangerous lintel will have it off with your feet.

NOTICE IN TOILET ON TRAIN, CHINA, 2007:

Do not use toilet while train is stabling.

This notice was corrected in preparation for the 2008 Olympics. It then read:

Do not use toilet while train is in stable.

Down Lintel!
Bad dog!

SIGN, GREECE:

Motorcycles for Red.

SIGN AT WILSON AIRPORT, NAIROBI, KENYA:

KENYA SCHOOL OF FLYLING
For Those Who Defy GRAVITY Safely.

PATTAYA, THAILAND:

Motorbytes for rent.

NOTICE IN TAXI, SHANGHAI, CHINA:

Psychos or drunkards without guardians are prohibited.

SIGN AT TRAIN STATION, ROME, ITALY:

Tickets must be obliterated.

Retail ructions

If you're one of those shoppers who gets annoyed at the inaccuracy of a 'five items or less' sign, you may want to avert your gaze at this point...

ON DOOR OF CLOSED SHOP, EGYPT:

I'm in the toilet.

BEAUTY SHOP, YANGON, BURMA:

Please, don't forget your valuable things in the toilet.

MASSAGE BUSINESS, CHINA:

Lord of the Ring Chinese Massage Center.

GYM, TOKYO, JAPAN:

Ret's Fitness!

WOMEN'S CLOTHES SHOP, CHINA:

Take free titty.

SALON, CHINA:

Foot care
Body care
Head care
Horny care.

SIGN OUTSIDE INDIAN HAIR SALON:

Super Saloon
Dye, fachial, messes and children cutting here.

SIGN, PRATAP PURA, INDIA:

Anus English Academy – no problem.

SOUTH GOA, INDIA:

Please do not park in front of the shitter.

SHOP SELLING BAVARIAN BEER MUGS, MUNICH, GERMANY:

We sell beer stains.

DUBAI, UAE:

A tailor in Dubai is called 'The In Trend', the labels in its garments reading 'TiT'.

NAME OF SPORTS SHOES SHOP, AIX-EN-PROVENCE, FRANCE:

Athlete's Foot.

SHOP, DALSTON, LONDON, UK:

Welcome the to shop.

This was then corrected to:

Welcome the shop.

ELECTRICAL APPLIANCE STORE, TOKYO, JAPAN:

May I ask a favor. Please refrain from bringing the goods before payment in the restroom.

ON A COSMETICS COUNTER, ROME, ITALY:

It is forbidden to trick yourself or prove the rosettes.

SIGN IN A DEPARTMENT STORE IN PERUGIA, ITALY, INDICATING THE LINGERIE SECTION:

Intimacy.

SIGN OVER ESCALATOR TO FEMALE CLOTHING DEPARTMENT, FLORENCE, ITALY:

Woman upstairs.

SIGN ABOVE DISPLAY OF DIGITAL CAMERAS, TENERIFE, CANARY ISLANDS:

BLOODY HELL OFFER.

BEAUTY SALON, CHINA:

Chinese Oil massage
European Oil massage
Trim the foot.

BEAUTY SALON, PHUKET, THAILAND:

A relaxing foot bath where you start with a special crime.

HOBBITS
SPORTS

BOOKSHOP, CHINA:

Sports and hobbits.

HOTEL SPA, CAIRO, EGYPT:

Pharaonic Body Warp
Body Warp (Seaweed).

SHOP IN MALLAIG, SCOTLAND, UK:

We can supply you with anything the West Highland weather can throw at you, including sunglasses.

SIGN ABOVE HOTEL JEWELLERY SHOP, THAILAND:

Porn gems.

SIGN, THAILAND:

Tattoo
Henna painting
Last 2 week temporarily.

SIGN ON AWNING OF SHOP, PARIS, FRANCE:

Alcools and stranger wines.

ON A DISPLAY OF 'I LOVE YOU ONLY' VALENTINE CARDS, USA:

Now available in multi-packs.

CLOTHING STORE, USA:

Wonderful bargains for men with 16 and 17 necks.

MEN'S CLOTHING STORE, TACOMA, WASHINGTON, USA:

15 men's wool suits – $10.00 – They won't last an hour!

SHOP, MAINE, USA:

Our motto is to give our customers the lowest possible prices and workmanship.

APPLIANCE STORE, KENTUCKY, USA:

Don't kill your wife. Let our washing machines do the dirty work.

CHINESE MEDICINE PRACTICE, SINGAPORE:

The practitioner offers treatments for the following complaints:

Knuckle disease
The knuckle ligament is harmed
The board is harmed in half a month
The fat cushion is strained
Fall and injure the department
The acute waist is sprained
Daily 9am–9pm. Pubic holiday – open.

Impenetrable instructions

You know what it's like with a new purchase – the excited rush to get home, the eager tearing away at the packaging, the anticipation as you take your new toy from its box – and then the puzzled face as you try to decipher the instructions…

MOBILE PHONE, CHINA:

Warning: do not follow these instructions may cause a fire, electric shock, damage or other damage

Do not throw, not disassembles or pierce Travel Battery.

ELECTRICAL WIRE CUTTERS, CHINA:

Before use, please read this instruction for god's sake and keep well... Please put on the ocular for use safe... Keep well for fear of danger.

MOP, CHINA:

On the base of innovative conception and dehydrate theory, it has poweful cleaning and 100% complete dehydrate effect which can not make your hands dirty. Now it has the following advantages: no waste physical strength, no need to plugging in, operate easily. Both man and children can use conveniently.

It can control the dry/wet percentage of the list automatically... Unique list fiber which can clean the dirty parts powerfully, and it would not scratch the floor and some other exquisite surface.

It adopts the technological design and can reduce the burden of hands/lumbar muscle which would not make you tired and body hurting. You only use it easily and make you do the homework quickly.

Clean the environment of your home like bathroom/ kitchen/living room/bedchamber easily. This one valued ten normal mops.

It can be used at home and some commercial or public space... wash the car and burnish and different parts.

DON'T USE MENTAL OR COARSE RAG TO WASH THE BUCKET IN CASE OF SCRAPING.

DON'T PUT THE EASY MOP DIRECTLY UNDER THE SUNSHINE. DON'T PUT THE EASY MOP CLOSE THE FIRE TOO MUCH IN CASE OF DAMAGE.

KIDS USE EASY MOP SHOULD BE KEPT WATCHING BY ADULTS.

FALLING FROM UPPER LEVEL IS FORBIDDEN.

PLS REMIND YOUR FAMILY (ESPECIAL OLDER AND KIDS), DON'T PLAY ON THE WET FLOOR, WHICH WILL LEAD TO SLIP.

TEAPOT, CHINA:

Made by handmade.

Product will be easy broken, please be careful to use.

Using limits: hot tea.

After pouring boiling water into the glass, temperature will rise up being very higher, be careful when the glass being burned.

Let glass keep away from the wet place.

Avoid hitting or dropping it from higher place.

Don't use in the dangerous situation, please always put on the flat.

Crack is the reason for glass broken.

Don't wash the glass with something hard or abrasiving it easily.

Don't use out of the product limits.

When washing, please keep space with others

GLUE, TUNISIA:

Can in a twinking glue to match the every kind of metals, rubber, handicraft product, car glass, etc.

METHOD OF USING:

1 Will first two the water of coalescanse things vamish rust the dust clearance is clean, and combine to beat to whet neat fit fogether the position. Because of its have no to fill the characteristic of the crevice.

2 Break the mouth of a bottle with pinprick, and lightly extrude a little amount glue even draw the cloth a the thing is superficial, fleetness with another a thing coalescence stick positive, bring pressure roughy 10 seconds, immediately glue to match.

3 If have to glue to connect not good, must afresh separate and remove the gumlayer, repetition above operation.

COLOUR PRINTER CARTRIDGE, BOUGHT IN UK:

Take out the pin from the lable which is sticked to the top-cover.

If the cartridge has several holes, please make sure all the holes are poked.

Attention Affairs... After poking the hole(s), please don't press or upside down the cartridge.

CAMERA, JAPAN:

Beware the weatherly swell.

TOY RACING CAR, COUNTRY UNKNOWN:

Enjoy racing once's limit, by skill, by speed, by taking once's limit, be tough, be strong, be a champion, are you rendr?

SPECIAL BAG USED FOR WASHING HORSE-RIDERS' CLOTHES, COUNTRY UNKNOWN:

After washing, any trapped horse-hair can be easily shaken out of the bag, ready for re-use.

SET-TOP BOX, COUNTRY UNKNOWN:

Please read this manual with sufficient carefulness and patience precede the connection and installation.

Advice you operate each function using the button.

Load the batteries to the groove of the remote controller and then enable you to operate the native.

When the picture the unexpected nonresponse happening please turn on the machine again.

Herein, what audio language is chosen indicates which owns the strong priority in broadcasting.

Fill a group of digits and then refill which.

The set channel will be enjoying when the installed time is up.

Any changes will not be noticed in advance. Our company reserves the right for the explanation of the discrepancy.

SHOES, CHINA:

Please put on the shoes with careful. You are liable to fall down by unsteady step.
Please don't told the back counter. It will be liable to put off you may be hurted.
Please put on the shoes according to using itself. The shoes are not match use itself make you hurted.

Please choose the shoes after knowing your foot size and character.

FEELING AN ITCH AND DERMATITIS: Don't put on the shoes promptly. The sickness may deepen.

Please pay attention to use in wearing bright socks. It will be liable to pollute the socks.

TICKET MACHINE, ITALY:

Insert the ticket.

Execute the payment.

LABEL ON ITEM OF CLOTHING, ITALY:

This item is brainchild of style research. The innovative design and the best material on the market confear at Kesly's item a particular vibration. Be grateful from all fashion victim.

KITE, COUNTRY UNKNOWN:

Never fly in thunder storms, rain or violate winds.
Never fly in crowded area since the hard crash can cause peoples hurting.
A park or beach is the idea flying sites.

MOP, COUNTRY UNKNOWN:

1. It fix automatically when twisting the fixer on mop makes it easy to change.

2. Made of cotton and yarn mixture, it is absorbable and not easy to twisted while sweeping, with wide sweeping area.

Damn!
INSTRUCTIONS

INSTRUCTIONS IN LAUNDRY, STUDENT HALLS OF RESIDENCE, RENNES, FRANCE:

Put the linen (to the ¾ of the drum)
Close the port hole
Regulate the cycle of was in
Introduce your detergent
Raise the number of the machine.

HANDSAW, COUNTRY UNKNOWN:

Suitable for wood, plastics and some metals. Not suitable for children under 36 months.

BATTERY FOR MOTORCYCLE, JAPAN:

Method of detoxify:

Outside: to wash by clear fresh water.

Inside: take a plenty of clear fresh water of cattle breast, well-distributed egg, or vegetable oil. Please sent to hospital at once.

FRENCH GRAIN MACHINE, WHICH AFTER SQUEEZING THE GRAIN ALLOWS IT TO FALL ONTO A CONVEYOR:

If you do not get a good humidity, you do not get a good falling down of the grain.

ITEM OF TECHNICAL EQUIPMENT, SPAIN:

The meter can be calibrated using a Tampon solution.

ON A PACKET OF BULBS, NETHERLANDS:

Stand six inches apart and make liberal water.

NOTICE RECEIVED WITH PRODUCT, CHINA:

This is not a toy and should be kept away from children made in China.

INSTRUCTION MANUAL, FRIDGE, GREECE:

Install the refrigerator at the low humidity and good air flow place.

Connect the power supply plug into an exclusive wall socket. You should insert a plug completely.

After the inside is cold well, store food. It takes approximately 4 hours for being fully cold. It may take a half day if the outside temperature is too hot.

Placing too much food will make the inside of the refrigerator not to be cool enough.

Wrapping food or putting it in the sealed case which it can keep its humidity and fresh.

Egg pocket. It can place eggs also turn the rear side to place the small pocket.

CAUTION:

Do not store bottles in a freezer compartment or a chilled case. It will become the cause of making you injured, if a bottle froze and explode.

Do not eat or drink smelling or color changing food. It might be the cause of sickness.

MODEL CAR, ITALY:

After applying transfers gently dab them with a damp sloth.

INSTRUCTIONS WITH POWER PLATE, TAIWAN:

Danger of life in case of non-respecting these advises.

Damages that have been caused by inappropriate treatment, conscious damage, wear or temptations of repairing are not included in the legal warranty period.

Take care that the training room has enough fresh air, but take care because vibration of the air can cause a cold.
Please wear comfortable cloth.
Because of the intensive vibrations you have to protect sensitive cloth, for example white socks or shorts, which get in touch with the vibration mat, with a pad or something similar.

Because of this reason it is really important to start really slowly with the training and to make brakes between and after the training.

OSCILLATING TOWER FAN, GREECE:

The fan should be put on the balance surface to avoid falling down.

Do not use in wet circumstance.

Do not insert anything into the inside body.

Stop using if any component is missed or the fan conk out.

SWING: Control oscillation or not once you press this button.

Do not use this product in serious dust or oil circumstance in order to avoid damage of the dust.
Make sure all the screw is fastened before you use it.
Please lay the fan on cool circumstance.

MOTORCYCLE MANUAL, GERMANY:

Running the engine without oil is punishable.

VEGETABLE CHOPPER, CHINA:

In order that the article has minced could be perfectly cut, knocked vigorously on the bud superior hand opened.

The most or less great number of knocks determines the fineness of cup.

For the cleaning, to pull the inferior bell and to release the recipient superior. Well to rinse the machine, if possible to the running water.

Re-assembly in senses inverts. All parts metallic are executed in a materials has the test of the rust.

HEAD-BAND, TAIWAN:

There is no standard to say tight or loose. It depends on the user's feeling by comfortable principle.

MODEL STEAM ENGINE, JAPAN:

This machine require no lubrication (except oil on all moving parts).

Garbling to the guests

The very best hotels provide a home away from home. The establishments featured in this chapter certainly achieve that – as long as your home is plastered with incomprehensible notices and error-strewn signs, that is...

BUDAPEST, HUNGARY:

For reasons of hygenie non-sliding mates for the bathtubes are posted at the reception.

CHÂTEAU HOTEL, THE DORDOGNE, FRANCE:

Offer a bowl of air to your seminars! The silence of one hotel in the countryside.

HOTEL IN NÎMES, FRANCE, WHOSE SWIMMING POOL IS OVERLOOKED BY FIRST-FLOOR BEDROOMS:

Dear Customers, In order to respect the touchiness of each one, we are asking you to wear your bra at the swimming pool.

HOTEL 1898, BARCELONA, SPAIN:

Airvex pillows – firmness to take care of your cervicals.

HOTEL, EGYPT:

Our public bar is presently not open because it is closed.

TRANSLATION OF 'BRA' ON LAUNDRY LIST, INDIA:

Breast hanger.

ALMATY, KAZAKHSTAN:

There is a bowel of fruit in each room.

SIGN AT SPANISH HOTEL ABOUT HOW TO GET IN AFTER 9PM:

You can not open the doors with your room number. Please do insert it at the automatic roomgiver for becoming your room number with the code for opening the doors. They will be noted on the ticket that the roomgiver gives you (don't forget it in the machine).

HOTEL WEBSITE, BELGIUM:

In the middle ages, an important road passed by this point... Historical documents teach us that a tavern was situated on our location... A lot later, the funtion of resting place for the horses fainted.

All rooms of double/twin and triple rooms dispose of an airconditioning.

You can cruise through our menu and beverage list by clicking here... Cozy bar with vaste choice of beers (about 25 species).

THE MENU INCLUDES:

Stew of pork cheeks with trappist beer.

PROMOTIONAL LITERATURE FOR TRIP TO KIEV, UKRAINE:

Kiev is the capital of Ukraine. It is the fantastic city full of history, beauty and culture! You will find the huge quantity of historical monuments of culture and religion in Kiev... And still you it is very tasty will feed in Kiev!

Accommodation includes staying in apartments in the centre of Kiev (BB: bad+breakfast).

HOTEL IN CROATIA:

Each guest is required personal identification card or passport register your stay at the hotel reception. Documents will be returned to his departure from the hotel.

If you want lunch, and lunch or dinner, please log on to the same reception when you check-in hotel.

Destruction is not allowed in and out of hotel rooms from inventory.

Each malfunctioning or defect in the room and possibly dissatisfaction service, please immediately register at the reception.

From 21.00pm to 7.00pm during the night of peace, so do not disturb other guests at the hotel.

Please free up room until 11.00am on departure day. Retention in the room after 11.00am, an additional charge conditioned room (daily rest). In the case of extending your stay please to announce the reception no later than 10.00 hours.

YOUTH HOSTEL, XINJIANG, CHINA:

We have good rooms, and the price is very cheap. Have three human lives and have four human lives, many human lives.

HOTEL IN FRANCE:

Breakfast... To order, thank you to phone reception.

You can get woke up by phone by calling at reception.

Television – the hotel is equipped with Canal Sat bouquet.

Pleasure and sincerity: I suggest in collaboration with this establishment a selection of fruit juices, nectars and jams... I look for growers respectful of their harvests... I personally validates each batch by attributing marks based on nose, mouth and texture.

Pets are not allowed in the breakfast.

Pets are
not allowed
in the breakfast

GUANGDONG, CHINA, WARNING OF SLIPPERY FLOOR:

Carefully slide.

HOTEL, USA:

The hotel has bowling alleys, tennis courts, comfortable beds, and other athletic facilities.

NOTICE ON JACUZZI, BALLATER, SCOTLAND, UK:

Please evacuate between the cycles.

HOTEL, BRUGES, BELGIUM, ADVISING THAT ITS BATHROOM LIGHT IS OPERATED BY A SENSOR:

Turns off approx. 15 minutes after last registered motion.

BATHROOM, FRANCE:

Do not throw kidney in the toilet.

HOTEL IN SHENYANG, CHINA:

Please obey the instructions of the hotel staff if it is on fire.

(The hotel's 'Do Not Disturb' lights are operated by switches labelled 'No bother'!)

NOTICE ABOVE TOILET, ROUEN, FRANCE:

Hunting of water located rear left electric toilet (press button round).

SIGN, JAPAN:

Please wash, disinfect and gargle the hand when it returns from going out.

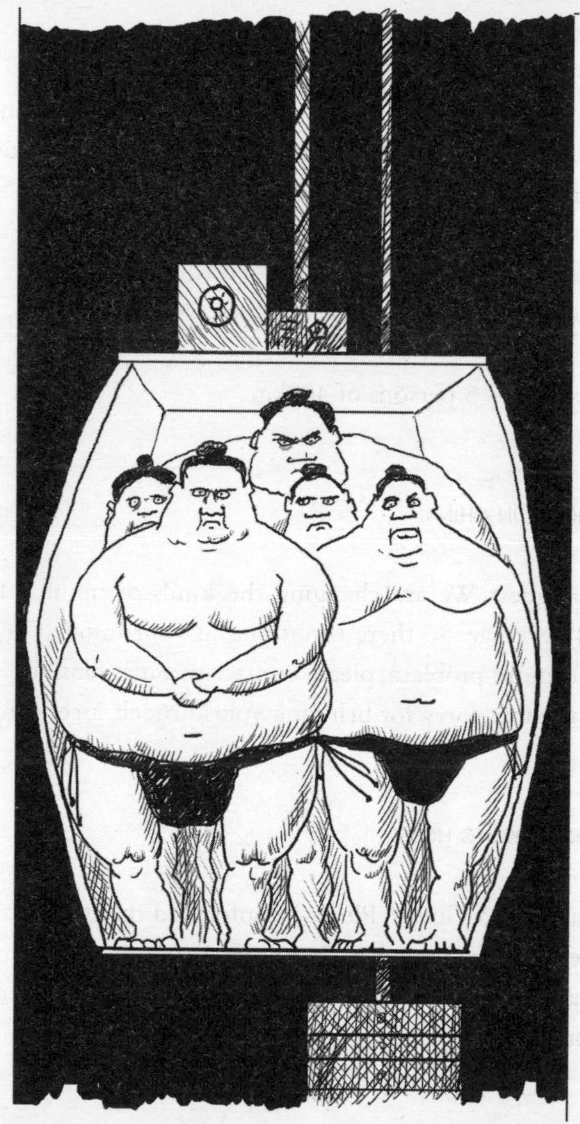

HOSTEL, BARCELONA, SPAIN:

We would be predicated if you could drink and eat in the Common Room but notice the Hostel does not provide a Kitchen to cook or store staff.

NOTICE IN HOTEL LIFT, SAINT HELIER, JERSEY, CI:

Max load – 5 persons of 400kg.

HOTEL IN CHINA:

Dear guest. We are changing the kinds of minibar food and beverage. So there is nothing in your minibar. If you need more problem, please contact us on extension 5. We are terribly sorry for bringing you so much inconvenient.

HONG KONG HOTEL:

Dear Valued Guests. Please be informed that the Japanese Television (Channel 6, 7, and 8) is out of order and is repairing now, any inconvenience caused is much appreciated.

NESSEBAR, BULGARIA:

Welcome to Beauty Aphrodite!

We offer the necessary for one unforgivable holiday of full value. You may choose between the relaxing massage next to the basin under the spoiling caress sea breeze or smarten up therapies in separate rooms.

BEIJING, CHINA:

The visitors would like to stay over night ought to be registered with the proper document.

VENICE, ITALY:

Forbidden the use of eletrical equipment with resistance on sight, or fed with solid, liquid or gaseous fuels.

HOTEL POOL, GREEK ISLAND OF NAXOS:

Lifebelts are only used in state of emergency.

HOTEL POOL, GREEK ISLAND OF SYROS:

The swimming pool is used only by the hotel's mates.

SIGN ON BOX, SYROS:

Answering coupon of opinion and suggestions.

HOTEL SPA, THAILAND:

Soak with enjoy dream romance milky blooming bath from coconut oil. Aroma blend of lavender and ylang ylang helps to radiant your skin and excellent nourishes.

Revitalize tired muscles, endurance against fatigue and bringing up joyful with happiness.

It's offering an excellent range of treatments by well trained and attentive Thai therapists. After visiting you may feel very pampered and moisturized.

HOTEL ROOM SAFE, SOUTH AFRICA:

1. To open the safe

a. Input the code (the original code set by factory is 1,5,9), and press 'A' or 'B', the green light on, please turn the key or knob in 5 seconds (if there is handle, please turn the handle first), and pull out to open the safe.

b. Each press the yellow light will flashing with the beep, indicating that microprocessor confirmed it. If the yellow light keep on flash with the beep means the code is wrong. Three times' wrong code will result the microprocessor refuse to accept the input for 20 seconds...

2. Close the safe

Close the door, and turn the key or knob (if there is handle, please turn the handle to the vertical place).

RESORT, ANTIGUA:

Our gardeners work deliquently.

CHENGDU, CHINA:

dear guset, none of the goods we provided in the guest room is present.

OXFORD, UK:

Face cloths, shower caps, dental kits, combs, shaving kits, sewing kits and sanity napkins available free of charge.

NOTICE, GERMANY:

Towels on Rail means: I'm use them again.

FRENCH PYRENEES:

Please inform the management of any defectives you find in this hotel.

ROME, ITALY:

The Minibar Service is at your disposal.

If you would like to have some drinks in the fridge, ask at the Reception Desk and we'll think about supplying it.

GOTHENBURG, SWEDEN:

The door is armed.

RIOM, FRANCE:

– Night auditor give you answers twenty fours hours on twenty fours hours.
– You have to give your laundry before seven o'clock pm and you get back in the morning by the flash bleue society.

CHAMONIX, FRANCE:

Breakfast 8.00 € per person. Extra of 1.50 € if been useful in room.

LIMASSOL, CYPRUS:

Bamber yourself with an upgrade.

BEIJING, CHINA:

Declaration:

Please don't worry if a fire is occurring. We hotel have owned succor scattering facilities to sure you transmitted safely.

Please follow the direction route to the information corridor and there safeguards will take you out to the security belts.

Point profess your excellency seat.

SAUNA TREATMENTS AVAILABLE AT A BEIJING HOTEL:

LINDA:
Suited crowd: the female whose slumber is not enough, and wants to take a good rest. Process: bath for 10 minutes – European style fragrant nursing for 60 minutes – suffocating for 5 minutes.

LUCY:
Suited crowd: the female whose skin is lack of moisture and also flabbily.

MILK:

Suited crowd: women who are down in spirits, which is caused by digestive system inordinate and endocrine maladjustment. Process... clear away horniness with the natural sea salt.

SAFLY:

Suited crowd: the male who have great working pressure, and lack of slumber.

KHORKINA:

Suited crowd: male who have not enough slumber, and need to have a good rest.

BANGKOK, THAILAND:

A surcharge of 650 Baht net would be charged to a hotel guest who has invited lady joiner or stranger to his room.

CANNES, FRANCE:

42 comfortable and hospitable rooms... All are sound-proof, air-conditioned, with satellite TV, magnetic anomaly detector.

324

NOTICE, GERMANY :

For earlier check-out please do not take the keys and put it in our postbox near the entrance door.

Welcome Rhein Tram/Train/Bus dayly ticket is at the reception for €2 per person to buy as our thanks to your choice.

HOTEL RECEPTIONIST TO GUEST, PARAGUAY, SOUTH AMERICA:

'You are just the sort of passenger we like to have at this hotel.'

PARIS, FRANCE:

We thank you for agreeing to put by ground the bathroom linen which you wish to make wash.

WASSERBURG, GERMANY:

To the dear house guests!
Please you pay only in *bar*!

For technical reasons we can no checks, visas, credit cards, no traveler checks, travel check, etc assume.

Fam. Greising requires a pleasant stay.

MONROVIA, LIBERIA:

Dear passengers, please be tiny when using ashtrays.

That's entertainment!

Writers and producers and artists spend their lives trying to entertain us. Some of them achieve this in ways they really weren't expecting...

PROGRAMME FOR JAPANESE BEATLES TRIBUTE BAND, EDINBURGH FESTIVAL, SCOTLAND, UK:

It's not too much to say that Beetles' 'hot', as if they were only devoting themselves to hotness itself... this year too, sublime yourselves straight into the heart of enthusiasm, even if some people say, 'They are too hot'.

THE VOICE-RECOGNITION SUBTITLING SERVICES ON LIVE TV CHANNELS SOMETIMES GET THINGS SLIGHTLY WRONG...

Actual comment: Health visitors are building relationships with parents.
Subtitle: Health visitors are building Russian ships with parents.

Actual comment: Boris Johnson is back for a second term as London Mayor.
Subtitle: Boris Johnson is bad for a second term as London Mayor.

Actual comment: [SWIMMER] It has been my dream since I was a little boy.
Subtitle: It has been my dream since I was a little buoy.

Actual comment: Welcome to the year of the horse.
Subtitle: Welcome to the year of the whores.

Actual comment: Katie Price.
Subtitle: Katie Piss.

Actual comment: Firefighters to deal with not just the fire, with people in the middle of the road, evacuating.

Subtitle: Firefighters to deal with not just the fire, with people in the middle of the road, ejaculating.

Actual comment: Five hundred badgers are set to be killed.
Subtitle: Five hundred actors are set to be killed.

Actual comment: Ed Miliband.
Subtitle: Ed Miller Band.

Actual comment: [DURING HER FUNERAL]: There will now be a moment's silence for the Queen Mother.
Subtitle: There will now be a moment's violence for the Queen Mother.

Actual comment: The Bulgarian population.
Subtitle: The bog Aryan population.

Actual comment: Those Mets have been doing their hot streak of late.
Subtitle: Those Mets have been doing their hot streak ovulate.

Actual comment: A former First Lady back at home, Nancy Reagan was...
Subtitle: A former fertile lady back at home, Nancy Reagan was...

Actual comment: Chances of rain today about 70 per cent.
Subtitle: Chances of rape today about 70 per cent.

Actual comment: Pigs love to nibble anything that comes into the shed, like our wellies.
Subtitle: Pigs love to nibble anything that comes into the shed, like our willies.

Actual comment: The Archbishop of Canterbury.
Subtitle: The arch bitch of Canterbury.

Actual comment: Rings of Saturn.
Subtitle: Rings of satin.

Actual comment: The players will mark the fact that tomorrow is Remembrance Sunday.
Subtitle: The players will mock the fact that tomorrow is Remembrance Sunday.

Actual comment: 500 exclusions issued [by a school].
Subtitle: 500 executions issued.

Actual comment: He was fouled by Evra.
Subtitle: He was fouled by a zebra.

◎ DESCRIPTIONS OF COMPUTER GAMES AVAILABLE FROM ONLINE APP STORE:

Explore Pablo's fantasy world. Watch the screenshot below and you will found this fantasy world are so excitement. Pablo will found several weapon to fight the foe. From axe, pick, hammer, morning star and sword. Each level has unique trap and obstacle. With 6 Boss Levels, Pablo will meet his foes with more and more difficult to beat as the level goes up.

The earth are in danger!!! Every asteroid, comet and alien thing in universe are turn against our earth. They are everywhere, the earth are being attack in every direction. With our at most technologies the President command you to prevent this apocalypse. 'Destroy every unknown subject that came near our earth, in all cost!!!' that's his command.

Now... you are our only hope, just use your finger and tap to the unknown subject.

When every super weapons are in full charge, you can use it any time.

Be careful of a very big asteroid!!!

BOARD GAME AVAILABLE IN CYPRUS:

Tiddleywings.

SONG ON A PIRATED DONNA SUMMER CASSETTE, TAIWAN:

'Hot Stiff'.

IN DUTCH CHILDREN'S BOOK, AIMING FOR 'TOILET':

Shit house.

THE FIRST VOLUME OF *LOST IN TRANSLATION* FEATURED AN EXTRACT FROM THE PROGRAMME FOR A GENOA OPERA COMPANY PRODUCTION OF *CARMEN*. IT CONCERNED ACT IV. SINCE THEN THE REST OF THE TEXT HAS BEEN BROUGHT TO MY ATTENTION:

Act I. Carmen is a cigarmakeress from a tobago factory who loves with Don Jose (Duet: 'Talk me of my mother').

There is a noise inside the tobago factory and the revolting cigar-makeresses burst into the stage. Carmen is arrested and Don Jose is ordered to mounting guard her but Carmen subduces him and lets her escape.

Act II. The Tavern. Carmen, Frasquito, Mercedes, Zuiniga, Morales. Carmen's aria ('The sistrums are tinkling'). Enter Escamillio, a balls-fighter. Enter two smuglers (Duet: 'We have in mind a business') but Carmen refuses to penetrate because Don Jose has liberated her from prison. He just now arrives (Aria: 'Slop, here who comes') but here are the bugles singing his retreat. Don Jose will leave and draws his sword. Called by Carmen's shrieks the two smuglers interfere with her but Don Jose is bound to dessert, he will follow into them (final chorus: 'Opening sky wandering life').

Act III. A rocky landscape, the smugler's shelter. Carmen sees her death in cards and Don Jose makes a date with Carmen for the next balls fight.

THEME PARK, BRUHL, GERMANY:

Slacky objects have to be put down before the ride.

US TV NEWS:

A caption during a US TV news programme labelled the interviewee as a 'pubic defender'.

PIRATED CHINESE DVD COPY OF *RETURN OF THE JEDI*:

This gathered to strengthen the contents' dependable with the reasonable sex, and improved the visual effect, and make the film have more to plane... Is interstellar war trilogy the in side make the personmost shake of a set. Hancuolou second princess of Li is from the bad luck inside the extrication, road gram become the 'Hopeless situation warrior' empress and their heavy also the plan hold the versa and intergalactic big war. For successfully complete the plan, they to try the real troops of training. In the galaxy, the imposing person of this group regroup for battle, deduced a field. The ream person is greatly terrified with the war!

LEEDS, UK ADULT MOVIE CINEMA, 1970s:

THE WIFE SWAPPERS (X)
Separate performances.

Another film was advertised as:

In French with English subtleties.

◎ SIGN BY FORTUNE-TELLING MACHINE, THAILAND:

To know your fortune, please put a coin in to the slot of box. See flashing light pointing to which number and then read predicting papers.

Recipe for disaster

The candles are lit, the relaxing music is playing in the background, your aperitifs have been ordered – now all you need to do is make sense of the menu...

RESTAURANT, ITALY:

If you want an outline or do you want to add to those already in conjunction with the main courses, salads are always available, tosco beans, tomatoes, vegetables redone in a pan.

AREZZO, ITALY:

Overcooked to the Chianti
Pig steak
Hot slices of bread
Leg of chiken hunter.

KARLOVY VARY, CZECH REPUBLIC:

Horses douvres.

MEDINA-SIDONIA, CÁDIZ, SPAIN:

Roast Alf Partridge
The Chef's Dick.

HOTEL RESTAURANT, ALBERTA, CANADA:

Tempt your palette...

Four more
Chef's Dick!

◎ ALMERÍA, SPAIN:

Fried potatoes, prickle and salad
Potatoes vapor, small fish, marinate and salad
Fried potatoes or salad and needle irons
Crumbs
Potatoes poor.

◎ MADRID, SPAIN:

Lawyer Foam.

◎ FRANCE:

Believed eggs.

◎ FISH RESTAURANT, BRITTANY, FRANCE:

[Monkfish in a marinière sauce] Rape, Sailor Style.

PROVENCE, FRANCE:

[Goat's cheese] Turd of goat.

SOUTHERN SPAIN:

Soup of the day – tequila.

THAI RESTAURANT, NORWICH, UK:

Cow Pat.

TOKYO, JAPAN:

There is a fish cooking which isn't being written here, too. Ask a waiter.

CHIANG MAI, THAILAND:

Chicken leg cocked in Thai Style.

PRAGUE, CZECH REPUBLIC:

The dainty farmer from Mexico
[Sliced peaches] Peaches from the execution.

BEIJING, CHINA:

Virgin chicken
Burnt lion's head.

CARPE DIEM LOUNGE CLUB, BARCELONA, SPAIN:

Humid chocolate cookie.

VILLEFRANCHE, FRANCE:

Salad, tomato, cogs (sprockets).

WAITER, CYPRUS:

'Would you like your eggs sprinkled?'

CHINESE RESTAURANT, HATFIELD, HERTFORDSHIRE, UK:

Charges is PER PERSON, sitting in the restaurant, you must inform staff if you do not intend to eat, only 1 extra person allowed sitting at the table without eating...

All food are for consuming in the restaurant.

All food are packed away at closing time.

The restaurant is covered on CCTV, which is connected to a management team; any unlawful damages or unsuitable behaviour to our restaurant and staff and any person consumed in the restaurant without paying, will be reposted to the police and will be prospected.

MEXICO:

Locust to the mayonnaise.

BAR, ROME, ITALY:

Jack Denials.

INDIAN RESTAURANT, LONDON, UK:

For parties of 12 or more we offer 10% discocunt

PERUVIAN RESTAURANT, USA:

Peruvian Special Chicken (Whole) – Never before served in the USA. Our roast chicken is specially brought here for the chicken eater lover. They look as a regular roast chicken. But, the different is our special ingredients, you must taste them before giving any comment.

GREECE:

Fish on the eyelid.

FRANCE:

Mules marinated.

CHINESE RESTAURANT, USA:

Steamed pork dumpings.

Another dish comes 'with spies'.

RESTAURANT, ITALY:

You are kindly requested not to reach for a table before going through the cashier.

SKI-RESORT, BAD KLEINKIRCHHEIM, AUSTRIA:

We serve for you:

Spicy from the noble turkey
Pink roasted calf bar peaks
Several roasted fish
Pork loin in a precious mushroom crust
Saddle of Rabbit in a vortex sheet.

Side dishes are titled 'Enclosures'.

The same resort's entertainment includes: '14.00 clock magic sled for ski midgets – free ski midgets'.

◌ AUSTRIA:

Valued Customers – It is not allowed to consume meals and drinks from our self-service restaurant!

◌ MASAI MARA GAME RESERVE, KENYA:

Cross tart
Dust pie
Toxic salad.

◌ CHINA:

Urinate beef boll rice noodles
Characteristic mixed rice noodles.

◌ CHINA:

Grilled sexual harassment.

CHINA:

Smoke turkey drumsticks
Smoke turkey wings
Smoke cow feet
Cow something
Salted pig feet
Salted pig tail.

CHINA:

Stuff: in palm treasure, crayfish, eight fingernail fish
Cook: Explodes, fries
Taste: Kim possible.

ASIA:

Fried horse crap with lime.

CHINA:

Row wipes the pear flowering quince soup
Chicken rude and unreasonable.

CHINA:

Pork loin in your juice.

SIGN HANGING FROM RESTAURANT CEILING, CHINA:

Fuck vegetables.

INDIA:

Get a free cock with each biryani.

INDIA:

Fresh visitable juice.

IN INDIAN RESTAURANT:

Kicheen room. Permission not aloud.

FOOD SHOP, ITALY:

This dry mushrooms is considered by experts the best in the word. Nowhere to be found.

ON THE MENU AT THE SOCHI, RUSSIA, 2014 OLYMPIC GAMES, 2014:

Cakes in ass.

KOH SAMUI, THAILAND:

Vagitarian pizza.

USA:

Dinner Special – Turkey $2.35; Chicken or Beef $2.25; Children $2.00.

BISTRO NEAR MUSÉE D'ORSAY, PARIS, FRANCE:

Uncooked, plate full.

MADRID, SPAIN:

Language of cow carpaccio
Gypsy chocolate arm
Cold coffee mouse with old ron
Cake of puffy pastry.

NAME OF CAFÉ ON THE ROAD FROM DUBAI TO ABU DHABI, UAE:

The Violent Flower Café.

PHUKET, THAILAND:

Fried serpent head
Fried morning glary
Five things soup in firepan.

ITALIAN RESTAURANT, UK:

Baby meat ravioli.

AMSTERDAM, NETHERLANDS:

Apple Pie with Wiped Cream.

ON A PACKET OF POLISH BISCUITS:

Store in temperature to 18 degrees C and relative humidity to 75% in dark place. Avoid large hestitation of temperature.

OHRID, MACEDONIA:

Baked crap
Fired trout.

SOFIA, BULGARIA:

Chicken soap
Cock appetizer.

TURKISH RESTAURANT, STOCKPORT, UK:

Potato wages.

SIGN AT POOLSIDE BAR, SPAIN:

If we abandon the terrace, please pay prior use it.

SALIMA, MALAWI:

Chicken in a coat.

HONG KONG:

Bowel of steaming rice.

BORDEAUX, FRANCE:

[Foie gras] Our special fatty liver half-cooked
Our vegetarian suggestion – cooked vegetables.

L'AMMIRAGLIO ('THE ADMIRAL') PIZZERIA, ROME, ITALY, MID-1970s:

Mushrooms Frying Pan
Kidney Bean of Oil
Stuffed Trousers

Characteristic house plate: Spit-Roasted Admiral
Beer: Great, Average, Small.

TAVERN, GREEK ISLAND OF NAXOS:

We have our own vegetable.

SEVILLE, SPAIN:

The chinstrap of cod saddled
The fished savages
The loin of major cattle
Salad of glutonies and prawn
Aubergine refills with sauce of cheese.

KUTNÁ HORA, CZECH REPUBLIC:

Pfefersteak roast on frictional kind prefer transfusion with cream sauce.

FRENCH HOTEL:

Bugger steak and chips
Roast mole.

CRETE, GREECE:

Reddening meat
Spleen omelet calf pluck
Bowels tomato special.

RESTAURANT IN THE BUDA HILLS, BUDAPEST, HUNGARY:

Soup of cock with liver dumplings
In red wine cooked cock
As a company we offer crispy bacon, sautéed mushrooms and small white onions. It's worth to mop up its gravy with fresh bread.

FRANCE:

Chopped Lamp
Whipper Cream.

CYPRUS:

Baked Potatoes with Feelings.

LUCERNE, SWITZERLAND:

Trout in Pistachios overcoat.

BUDAPEST, HUNGARY:

Potato and cheese doughnuts with a garden salad infatuated with mint
Tenderloin mignons with a hazelnut sauce with a balmy rise and buttercorn
Meager mushroom stew with small dumplings.

SOPOT, POLAND:

Breaded in gentle cake, throw onto pepper cayenne
Cakes of Crabs
Small round cat Pork fillets.

HOTEL, CAGLIARI, SARDINIA:

Fillet of horse to the grate
Ham and Fig trees
Three of a kind of smoked mixed of sea
Bits in Brine
It gleans to the grate
Fried mixed of the Gulf
It gleans to the Calamosca (with fruits of the sea)
Big Prize.

RESTAURANT, GREECE:

Fish, chips and piss.

RESTAURANT, GREECE:

Bowels in spit.

Ha! Ha! Look, it says "Angry fish" here.

◌ LAKE TRASIMENO, PERUGIA, ITALY:

Angry fish.

◌ MOSCOW RESTAURANT:

Sturgeon cooked with spit.

◌ ROME, ITALY:

Spaghetti with clamps.

◌ ALICANTE, SPAIN:

Hay and straw.

◌ CAFÉ, GERMANY:

Re: price of tea: To change from cup to can, you must one euro sixty more pay
We have also diabetes cake.

PARIS, FRANCE:

Apple Grumble.

HIMACHAL PRADESH, INDIA:

Finally chopped vegetables.

SALAMANCA, SPAIN:

Cod in sauce of the grandmother.

CAFÉ, MURCIA, SPAIN:

Tea of Flavors (... fruit of the passion tea)
Short and concentrated coffee
Typical Spanish Sweet (Ribs)
Beaten of Chocolate, It mills
Refilled olives
Marriage
Cake of meat
Dressed loin
Soft drink Without Spring
Sailor's blouse.
The menu adds:

Besides, may we also suggest you:
Letters we have other letters
Ice cream letter – it enjoys our ice creams and glasses
Letter of Internacional Beers – Joint party our passion by the beer
Service and taxes including.

CZECH REPUBLIC:

Spelled Coffee.

ITALY:

Pasta to the angry one
Tortellini to the vain juices
Noodles to the porky mushrooms
Butterflies to the farmer
Laughed sea.

SAINT-OMER, FRANCE:

Good-looking net of pig
Mouse of lamb stewed to the goatherds
Greedy coffee.

RESTAURANT, SWITZERLAND:

Stewed cockerel in red wine sauce.

ITALIAN RESTAURANT, VIETNAM:

Crappy suzet.

OUTSIDE RESTAURANT, GREECE:

Try the local cuisine and traditional sweets, enjoy the aromas of fresh seafood while being cooked.

CAFÉ, GREECE:

Tea and berries shaked with milk
Market person in charge

Stuff potato
Drought beer.

CANTEEN MENU, GERMANY:

Low Fit Dish – Irish Lamb Stew.

RECIPE IN A FREE BOOKLET FROM A DANISH SUPERMARKET CHAIN:

Creamy Snowcrap in a crispy basket.

DENMARK:

Rabbit with herpes and wine.

GREEK ISLAND OF AEGINA:

Code with garlic sauce.

GREECE:

Eggs served with toast, white or brawn.

SAINT-VALLIER-DE-THIEY, PROVENCE, FRANCE:

Cuntry salad.

LAKE COMO, ITALY:

Soup of the Lake.

ANGKOR WAT, SIEM REAP, CAMBODIA:

Screambled eggs
Garlic break.

KAS, TURKEY:

Lamp shank
Lamp stew
Lamp casserole
Leg of Lamp (for two person).

◎ SANDWICH SHOP, ATHENS, GREECE:

Buckets [baguettes].

◎ KEBAB SHOP, PATRAS, GREECE:

Salad rustic
Banger rustic
Pork issue.

◎ FROM VARIOUS SOUTH AMERICAN MENUS:

Special meat accompanied by potato to the oven
Rice of the house and salad to the election
Fillet portion to the iron with bacon and adorned of butter, blow
Pickled bread chicken.

◎ BOLIVIA:

Sandwich gives chicken
Broth gives chicken
Prostrate fried salads to the pleasure he/she gives the victim.

Meat gives head sausage cheese egg olives garnish
Chop gives head rice or noodles potatoes
You dull coffee.

AGUAS CALIENTES, PERU:

ENTRANCE
Avocado to the queen

MEAT
Typical
Beefsteak to the poor
Beefsteak whit pure of pope
Coiled of meat.

GERMANY:

Two clods with salt potatos, green salad and a sharp sauce.

MADRID, SPAIN:

Ear to the plate (pig)
Squids to the Roman
Razors to the Plate

Swimming Crabs
Domestic Croquettes
Moorish Thorn
Brave Potatoes
Octopus to the Galician
Chops of Sucking
Cheeks with Mushrooms in Green Sauce.

AYIA NAPA, CYPRUS:

Cheeseburger with cheese.

BANGKOK, THAILAND:

Fried rice the pork ferment
Friend rice the sea.

CAFÉ, ISTANBUL, TURKEY:

Chicken tits – hot as hell.

NAME OF RESTAURANT, GRAVOIS MILLS, MISSOURI, USA:

Big Dick's Halfway Inn.

CHINESE NOODLE BAR, ALBANY, WESTERN AUSTRALIA:

With the mixture of seafood, thick egg noodles are tossed with prawns, crabs, ticks, shrimps... A delicious taste we can all bow to agree.

With this dish, enjoyment only comes afterwards.

Taking the tasty satay sauce, combine it with all the fresh veggies: over a quick stir-fry into the hot wok with thick egg noodles, it's a meal's on the edge of your mouth.

Four in One-pack – a great mix for the adventuress type of people.

BUDAPEST, HUNGARY:

Winged dishes.

ROME, ITALY:

Envelopes with cheese
Bakery potatoes.

LISIEUX, FRANCE:

Salad of hot goat
The piece of the butler butcher
Mustard coloured small sausage made of chitterlings to the ancient
Milfoil of twerps to the apples
String bag of harvest bug barbet on field of leeks
Pot of tremendous dips to the sauce
Thigh rabbity hunter fashioning
Miller's wife field
Fishy soup.

BULGARIA:

Fumigated cheese.

PORT GRIMAUD, FRANCE:

Greedy salad
Crusty of goat het as a chaplain
Melon with Oporto and its believed ham
Tagliatelli and its bolognaise the old one
Paving stone kangaroo and its sauce.

ISTANBUL, TURKEY:

Kids in spit.

MANHATTAN, NEW YORK, USA:

Lunch special – $6.95 – Come with soup or Thai salad.

RESTAURANT AT SAINT PETERSBURG PULKOVO AIRPORT, RUSSIA:

Language beef and vegetables [beef tongue and vegetables].

PRAGUE, CZECH REPUBLIC:

Homemade Graves with onions.

RUSSIA:

Pelmeny wish soul cream.

MOSCOW, RUSSIA:

Piglet milk.

NAME OF FRANCHISE AT FARO AIRPORT, PORTUGAL:

Burger Me.

SPAIN:

€18.00 Set menu (€10.00 for children having small potions).

GREECE:

Cretan smocked pork meat
Burning cheese
Pens with basil pesto and parmesan.

Sell, sell, sell

Advertising and promotion are all about grabbing the reader's attention. Some organisations do that in more ways than one...

TOURIST ADVERTISEMENT, CROATIA:

Porec – The Mediterranean in the Hearth of Europe.

TAILOR, CHINA:

Fat Guy furrery tailor made keepin good repair.

BANNER ABOVE BUSINESS PREMISES IN CHINA, OBVIOUSLY WRITTEN USING A COMPUTER PROGRAM:

'Translate server error'.

Similarly, another had a banner reading 'Computer error'...

... and a Chinese zoo had an information panel reading: 'Englishenglishenglishenglishenglishenglishenglish...'

WINDOW CLEANER, UK:

We clean

Residential windows
Shop windows
Office windows
Conservatives.

TOURIST SIGN, INDONESIA:

Thangs you for come to fisiting us.

HANDWRITTEN NOTICE, CHINA:

Engish lessons! You call now!!!

LAUNDRY, USA:

We do not tear your clothing with machinery. We do it carefully by hand.

CLASSIFIED ADVERTISEMENTS FROM VARIOUS LOCAL NEWSPAPERS, USA:

2 female Boston Terrier puppies, 7 wks old, Perfect markings, 555-★★★★. Leave mess.

Lost: small apricot poodle. Reward. Neutered. Like one of the family.

A superb and inexpensive restaurant. Fine food expertly served by waitresses in appetizing forms.

For sale: an antique desk suitable for lady with thick legs and large drawers.

Four-poster bed, 101 years old. Perfect for antique lover.

Now is your chance to have your ears pierced and get an extra pair to take home, too.

For Sale: three canaries of undermined sex.

For Sale: eight puppies from a German Shepperd and an Alaskan Hussy.

Great Dames for sale.

Have several very old dresses from grandmother in beautiful condition.

Tired of cleaning yourself? Let me do it.

Dog for sale: eats anything and is fond of children.

Vacation Special: have your home exterminated.

Get rid of aunts: Zap does the job in 24 hours.

Toaster: a gift that every member of the family appreciates. Automatically burns toast.

Sheer stockings. Designed for fancy dress, but so serviceable that lots of women wear nothing else.

Stock up and save. Limit: one.

We build bodies that last a lifetime.

For Rent: 6-room hated apartment.

Used Cars: Why go elsewhere to be cheated? Come here first!

Modular Sofas. Only $299. For rest or fore play.

Our bikinis are exciting. They are simply the tops.

Auto Repair Service. Free pick-up and delivery. Try us once, you'll never go anywhere again.

Mixing bowl set designed to please a cook with round bottom for efficient beating.

Semi-Annual after-Christmas Sale.

And now, the Superstore – unequaled in size, unmatched in variety, unrivaled inconvenience.

We will oil your sewing machine and adjust tension in your home for $1.00.

FROM VARIOUS SITUATIONS VACANT/EMPLOYMENT COLUMNS, USA:

Wanted: hair-cutter. Excellent growth potential.

Wanted. Man to take care of cow that does not smoke or drink.

Wanted: unmarried girls to pick fresh fruit and produce at night.

Our experienced Mom will care of your child. Fenced yard, meals, and smacks included.

Wanted: 50 girls for stripping machine operators in factory.

Wanted. Widower with school-age children requires person to assume general housekeeping duties. Must be capable of contributing to growth of family.

Wanted: chambermaid in rectory. Love in, $200 a month. References required.

C.V.

Man, honest. Will take anything.

3-year-old teacher needed for pre-school. Experience preferred.

ADVERTISEMENT FOR HAINAN ISLAND (CHINA) IN HONG KONG TRAVEL AGENCY:

Looking for beach & shinesun? Hainan Island enjoy all feeling!

ADVERTISEMENT FOR SPIRITUAL HEALER, GREECE:

Over 15 years experience no matter what your problems are I can help you solve the most difficult once in the fastest way than any one does even when you have been disappointed by other spiritualists. I can bring the loved once more than they are before. I can bring unknown one in love. I also give powerful talisman for protection. Impotency sexual court case exams carrier. Successful business depression and many other things.

SLOGAN FOR JUICE DRINK, CHINA:

Everyone, everywhore.

WEDDING HIRE SERVICE OFFERED BY MENSWEAR SHOP, SOUTH AFRICA:

The suit are as important as the wedding dress and represent your style, personality and the image you want to perceive to your love one for years to come, therefore it is important to feel as comfortable and style full in your own special way... and please, don't try to match up with the serviettes.

FLORIST, SOUTH AFRICA:

Pretty flowers. Let us help you take them away. It can be anything you need to solve like arranging weddings, flower requirements, rid people's troubles.

TOURIST BROCHURE, PORNICHET, FRANCE:

At Pornichet people both big and small have the choice between attractions... for the loyal race track lovers, Pornichet does things well, its race track offers 4 daily races and 15 nighty races.

ADVERTISEMENT FOR AN ATHENS TOILET-CLEANING FIRM:

The advert boasts that it 'specialises in cleaning, disinfection and flavouring your toilet'.

Another company in Athens boasted about opening a new 'flagfish' store.

ADVERT FOR A MENSWEAR COMPANY IN A GERMAN NEWSPAPER:

GET THE BEST BEFORE ANOTHER ONE GETS!

ADVERTISEMENT FOR GUEST HOUSE, HIMACHAL PRADESH, INDIA:

Stay homely!

SIGN OUTSIDE A UK PUB:

Only 2 meals for £5.

SIGN OUTSIDE A GREEK TAVERN:

It would be very happy, because you have a very nice one and pleasant interlocutors are.

SKI CENTRE WEBSITE, SARAJEVO, BOSNIA-HERZEGOVINA:

It's our pleasure to present you Jahorina, the snow queen, the mountain which was the housewife of Winter Olympic Games in 1984.

NEWSPAPER ADVERTISEMENT FOR AN ACADEMY IN EDINBURGH, SCOTLAND, UK:

NUTURING INDIVIDUAL ACHIEVEMENT.

TOURIST SIGN, CHINA:

Welcome for coming!

SIGN IN INDIA:

Sexologist. Only on Sundays.

FLYER STUCK TO LAMPPOST IN CALAIS, FRANCE:

SUPER HANKY PANKY.

ADVERTISEMENT FOR A DANCE EVENING AT A CAMPSITE IN SOUTHERN SPAIN:

Come for all sorts of dancing with the strangers.

HERBAL FOOTBATH

SIGN OUTSIDE A HEALTH FOOD SHOP, FINCHLEY, LONDON, UK:

Don't let your feet kill you. Try our herbal footbath.

CLASSIC CAR MUSEUM, ATHENS, GREECE:

You will meet the all History of Automobile
50 Infrequent cars in show condition and complete functional of VIP owners that left history in our place.

BROCHURE FOR A MEDIEVAL TOWN, FRANCE:

Welcome to our middle-aged town.

AMERICAN CAR WEBSITE:

Our Colgan or Porsche factory bras are designed to protect your car from animals, meteorites, small children, and other common road debris.

CAFÉ, DRESDEN, GERMANY:

In the year 1992 the family Eisold transferred the Café Toscana and invested much time and money, in order to help the old Grand lady of the Dresdener café landscape again to old beauty. The entire old explosive growth house was reorganized original-faithfully and with much love. The traditional exempt private company – the bakers shop and confectionary Eisold – existed now in third Generation. In the Café Toscana one can enjoy today the baking art of experience for many years and proven prescriptions.

We are pleased about your visit!
The history of Café Toscana:

The time of origin: Friedrich Louis Kohler bought the just now finished house at the corner of the urban house line at the old village meadow of Blasewitz, the today's Schillerplatz to 1897, and furnished therein a coffee bar. 1906 took over then the very successful Confectionary Master Hugo Zimmermann the business, extended it by a baking room and designated its café somewhat provocatively after the Crown Princess Luisa von Toscana, which had fled in December 1902 of the saxonian yard.

The time of blossom: From the outset the café ran unusually well – so well the fact that the first operator did not even find for many years the time to visit its mother and her instead according to Blasewitz invited. Under Heinrich Zimmermann the son-in-law of Kohler's, the café arrived at the good reputation, which admits it over the borders of Blasewitz outside made. However one whispered that Kohler was to have spend the money with full hands again.

The time of GDR: The wedding of the GDR was at the same time the decline of the Café Toscana. Also in the time of the goods scarceness the Toscana was nevertheless over many years a good address. Gradually the built volumes worsened. So for example the winter garden had to be closed and the baking room to be outsourced. Also the old fan club was missing with the time.

NAME OF TRAVEL COMPANY, CAIRO, EGYPT

Gabry Inter Travel Service, or GITS.

COMPUTER GAME, JAPAN:

This web game is to use the mouse to feed Wind powder, the powder dance to enjoy the game.

NAMIBIA TOURIST BOARD, AFRICA

A brochure published by the Namibia Tourism Board included a reference to 'elephants gambling along'.

RESTAURANT, LIMASSOL, CYPRUS

In *Still Lost in Translation* we savoured the publicity emails sent out by a restaurant in Limassol, Cyprus. They're still at it...

The Autumn is already there and very soon winter is arriving, the pans and cutleries of the French Restaurant La Maison Fleurie in Limassol started to danse again in a very crazy mood!! From every corner of the restaurant you can smell the flavours of a delicate cuisine and of fines products & ingredients! The restaurants enters in the winter timetable now and inform everybody that Lunch time is on again! From deer in Red wine of Cahors, Fricassee of Grouse to Duck Confit in Wild Mushrooms of French Province is all you wish to know & taste! Take a Lunch break from your office work, seduce in this gourmet frenzy your collagues and clients and live a Dejeuner in Style!!!

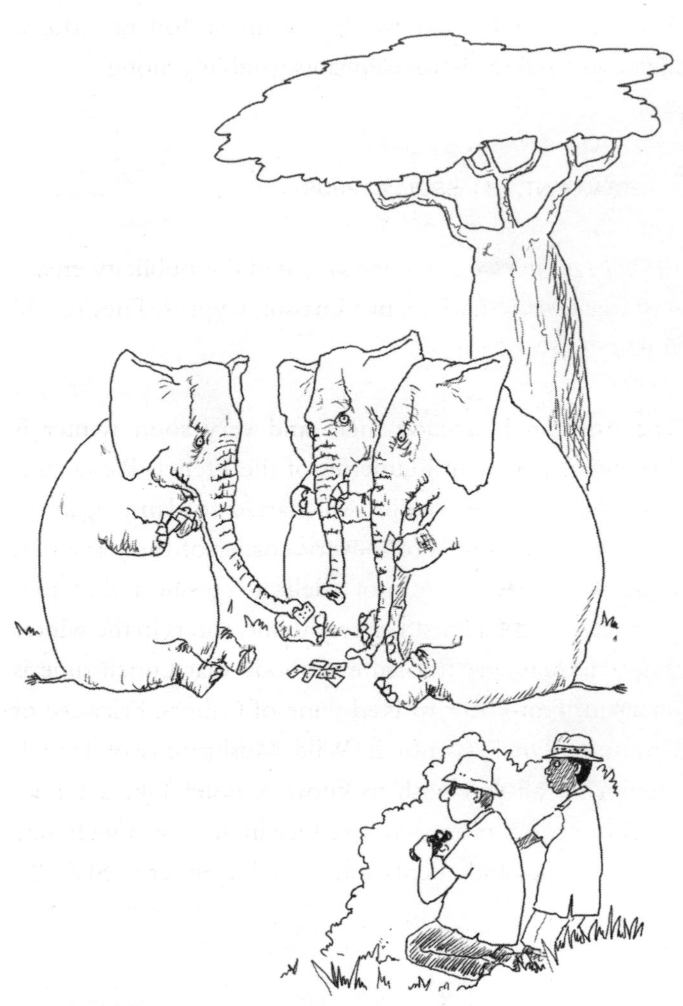
Sell, sell, sell

EBAY DESCRIPTION OF DIGITAL CAMERA, JAPAN:

The camera itself has not belonged.

TOURIST BROCHURE, LAOS:

Dimish the seriousness of yourselves in the Laos.

ON THE WEBSITE OF A CHINESE PERFUME COMPANY:

Shandong Yaroma desires the pleasure cooperation with you.

ADVERTISEMENT FOR AN ENGLISH TEA ROOM, CYPRUS:

Scons jum and cream, served in old English china, in a quent village admosphere.

BROCHURE FOR COSMETIC MEDICAL PROCEDURE, ITALY:

This injection technique is used mainly in the fragile areas of the face subjected to tension: rooster paws, wrinkles of cheeks and labial corners.

Packaging can be a tricky issue. It's often claimed these days that a product 'does what it says on the tin'. With these products you sincerely hope that isn't true...

NAME OF BEAUTY PRODUCT, CHINA:

Face Bashing.

ON A PACKAGE CONTAINING METAL PLIERS, A METAL SCREWDRIVER AND A METAL HANDSAW, CHINA:

Manicure Set.

TOOTHBRUSH BOUGHT IN SYDNEY, AUSTRALIA:

Quality bristles to clear away the crack dirt, result is special well, the bristles can achieve clean and massage your teeth dual efficacy. Grasp strengthened anti-slip type rubber handle and the special grasp and anti-slip design, gives you comfort and firm feelings.

TAG ON SHIRT BOUGHT IN AUSTRALIA:

Looking fantastic and comfortable while wearing. Wear for activities that stirs enthusiasm.

BRAND NAME OF FIREWORKS, CHINA:

Thunder Crap.

GUARANTEE SUPPLIED WITH PAINTED PAPYRUS, EGYPT:

We are very happy to present you this papyrus. The plant grew on the edge of the Nile and was trated in our factory, it has the same qualities. Both chemical and physical the ancient papyrus had. On the light you can see the horizontal and vertical lines and the dark cells that differentiate from any other. You can write on it by means of pens, water colour it can be rolled and its long life makes it more valuable by the passing time.

ON A PACKET OF SUGAR, CHINA, REFERRING TO THE COMPANY:

ENOUGH OLD
ENOUGH SPECIALIZED.

BOX OF ARTISTS' PASTELS, CHINA:

The MASTERS PASTEL that adopts the latest technology produces have the characters of vivid shade, durable, innocuous, no easybreak, bright pen body, rolling up chops and wiping.

TIN CAN, CHINA:

Bottled water.

PACKET OF JACKFRUIT CRISPS, VIETNAM:

These products have also a good smelling and crunchy feature which gives a good taste and provide more nutritive facts, vitamins, mineral salt necessary to the organism and protecting from the extra glucoza.

PACKET OF SUGAR, IRELAND:

According to the advice on the packet, the manufacturers claim that the product 'reduces feelings of depravation'.

3D PUZZLES DEPICTING A BUTTERFLY AND A SPIDER, CHINA:

'Butterfly Helena' is made of Brazil and Peru. There is little now there. It is called the most beautiful in the world. It not only has a rounded body, but also brightness and discolour. Sometimes is dark blue, and sometimes is shallow blue. It looks like jewel on the fly, more honorable and charming.

'Spider Rose' is made of the forest in South America. There are full of drak red hair on its body. It belongs one of the cavern spider. It is virulence.

Use hand and head – Training kid's flexible for their proportion on the hands and eyes. Develop them imagination ability. Make a teaching fairyland.

Design munificent – It can be assemblaged detached over and over, and looks like vertiable. It needn't any assist tools.

Perfect in workmanship – Materials are daintiness. Safety and slightly. Full of colour printing.

◎ BUCKET, COUNTRY OF ORIGIN UNKNOWN:

Into Pail
Created for Your New Liftstyle
Get into Pail.

◎ PACKET OF BISCUITS, CHINA:

Two Varieties Sand Cookies.

◎ KITCHEN CLOTH, CHINA:

Grease removing – softness – bibulousness.
No plasm – no shrinking – high strength.

Sewing at warp-winse and crosswise... it features solid and deformation with the best using effect.

The inside and outside layers of it are prepared scientifically with the features of better softness and bibulousness as well as better effect in grease removing and stronger in strength. It doesn't go moldy, rotten and unhealthy even in the water for a long time.

JAR OF RASPBERRY JAM, USA:

Tastes like Grandma.

ON A CARTON OF ORANGE JUICE, SERBIA:

CLOUDY FRUIT NECTAR.

BODY CREAM, ITALY:

This cream is particularly advised to subjects with sensitive and reactive skin to bad external spurs.

Anyone seen my teeth?

A sign of things to come

As we navigate our way around the modern world there are all sorts of signs to help us out. They tell us where to go, how to behave, what to do and what not to do. Many of them are helpful and clear. Then there are the other ones...

MOSQUE, ISTANBUL, TURKEY:

Do not enter with short, Bermuda and mini-skirt.

PAYPHONE, THAILAND:

If you use the pay phone I f***ing kill you but you may use pay phone if wish.

BAR, ROME, ITALY:

Please use the arse-tray for your fags.

MUSEUM, MYCENAE ARCHAEOLOGICAL SITE, GREECE:

Visitors to this site are requested to be decently clad.

GREAT WALL OF CHINA:

Please don't carve abitrarily on the Great Wall. Protect one brick and one stone consciously...

Please walk carefully on abrupt slope and dangerous way. Don't run and pushes to pash violently and the laugh and frolic...

MILITARY CHECKPOINT, EGYPT:

Chickpoint.

CAFÉ IN VIENNA FLUSS GARDENS, 1960s:

Consummation obligatory!!

NOTICE TO THOSE VISITING THE WALLS OF THE MEDIEVAL VILLAGE OF MONTERIGGIONI, TUSCANY, ITALY:

Attention: the unprovided ticket visitors an administrative sanction will be applied.

He is forbidden to rise and lean of the walls out.

He had forbidden to spout or to abandon rubbish to the ground.

NEAR NGORONGORO CRATER, TANZANIA:

Be aware of invisibility.

Ooops ...!
Sorry!

SIGN, CHINA:

For the sake of everyone's enjoyment please do pick the flowers.

FRENCH CAMPSITE:

SWIMMING POOL: to respect for the displayed recommendations has know:
Obligatory bath briefs
Games of balls and bullets forbidden
Forbidden palms
Sault, let's dive, hustles are forbidden
Before penetrating on the beaches, borrow the pediluve.

BY CHINESE CABLE CAR:

Don't make skies fall down!

ZOO, PUNE, MAHARASHTRA, INDIA:

Please do not Annoy, Torment, Pester, Molest, Worry, Badger, Harry, Harass, Hackle, Persecute, Irk, Rag, Vex, Bother, Tease, Nettle, Tantalise or Ruffle the Animals.

OUTSIDE CLOTHES SHOP, AMSTERDAM, NETHERLANDS:

You will never be more than you are naked.

ROAD SIGN, HERTFORDSHIRE, UK:

No vehicles please. Wet flood.

WATERWAY, GERMANY:

Attention: Limit interdicted waters to the navigation not signalled.

HISTORIC WATCHTOWER, SPAIN:

Visitors removing stones will be hardly punished.

LIFT, FRANCE:

The not accompanied children can not use the elevator.

SIGN, CHINA:

Please only pee here or you will be punished.

ABOVE FIRE-EXTINGUISHER, CHINA:

Hand grenade.

NEAR RIVER, CHINA:

Take the child.

Fall into water carefully.

HOSPITAL WAITING ROOM, CHINA:

Dying right here is strictly prohibited.

SIGN, CHINA:

A man toilet buries you to external right side stairs.

TOILET, CHINA:

Don't stampede.

ANOTHER TOILET, CHINA:

This is what I've always wanted to talk to you:

Urinating into the pool – you are the best.

DANGEROUS HILLSIDE PATH, CHINA:

Beware of missing foot.

DANGEROUS HILLSIDE PATH, CHINA:

Beware of missing foot.

SIGN NEAR INDIAN BUILDING SITE:

Caution! Heavy erection under progress.

TOURIST SITE, THAILAND:

Do not entry.

ON LEGEND OF TOURIST MAP, THAILAND:

Are you here?

TOILET, CHINA:

Please do not shit in the toilet.

SIGNS AT IGUAZU FALLS, ARGENTINA:

Take a careful

Do not overtake the bannister.

MUSEUM, SANYA, HAINAN, CHINA:

Do not touch and pay for damaging.

HOSPITAL, ENGLAND, UK:

Have you tried our staff canteen? Our prices are more than reasonable.

SHOWERS, FRENCH CAMPSITE:

Dear Campers – please leave your shoes to the outside of showers to see the health of sol. Thanks to all.

TOILET, BUCHAREST OTOPENI AIRPORT, ROMANIA:

Please keep cleaning.

SIGN, CHINA:

If you would like to join us, rubbish will never be homeless.

SKI RESORT, BULGARIA:

Exit from the marked and guarded ski slopes is hazardous for your health and life. In close proximity there are rocky rapids and avalanche chutes. The responsibility is entirely at your misfortune!

ON THE BACK OF A TOILET DOOR, FETHIYE, TURKEY:

Please do not put paper or any other staff down the toilet.

ON THE DOOR OF A PUBLIC WASHROOM, GOVERNMENT OFFICE, INDIA:

Please use flash. Close tap before leave.

TOURIST SITE, THAILAND :

Tour. A revival of the Khao Sok National Park. The guides speak english very well for every trip. We show you the beauty of our countryside. We have licensed tours and a good insurance. The law must follow the rules.

HOSPITAL, GREEK ISLAND OF SYROS:

Are U afraid that you have the new flu? Telephone in the 22813 and speak with the being on duty doctor.

DISABLED TOILET, THAILAND:

Toilet for cripple.

THAILAND:

No give food monkey.

Do not feed the wildlife and be careful danger!

Beware a monkey steal your belonging.

TOILET, FARNHAM, ENGLAND, UK:

ABSOLUTELY NOTHING DOWN THE LOO.

SIGN AT ITALIAN MOTORWAY CAFÉ ENTRANCE:

Mistrust abusive vendors.

SIGN ON DOOR, CHINA:

Please push out for exist.

SIGN ON FENCE NEXT TO CANAL, SHANGHAI, CHINA:

No shinning.

MONT ST-MICHEL, FRANCE:

Don't risk you in the bay during the tide. This can surprise you at each time.

MUSEUM, GERMANY:

Using the stairs, bars and platforms at own risk! The entire area is videosupervised. In cases of vandalism we reserve ourselves refunding an announcement!

ROAD SIGN, ITALY:

Beware of children.

SIGN, CHINA:

Building asks a smoked visitor in the outside smoking section that you cannot smoke in.

SIGN ON GRASS, CHINA:

Please do not disturb me.

SIGN IN LIFT, PAKISTAN:

Press up to go up
Press down to go down.

SIGN, CHINA:

Having fun prohibited.

IN A TOILET, CHINA:

The free toilet paper
Please treasure the use.

ON LOW ROOF, CHINA:

Bump the head care sully.

A sign of things to come

SIGN ON THE GREEK ISLAND OF LEFKADA, REPRODUCED HERE IN ITS ENTIRETY:

We thank you for the comprehension.

SIGN AT POOL BAR, ALSO IN LEFKADA, GREECE:

All the swimmers should be healthy and clean, to behave decently and use well the installations.

People suffering from dermal diseases, do not become acceptable.

People that have extensive exdores, open pustules and lesions, should avoid the swimming so that to avoid infections.

Each swimmer before coming to the space of swimming pool owes to go to the bathroom for urination and then to have a bath of cleaness.

It is prohibited the effervescent and dangerous games at the space of various installations.

People who are not compromised with the regulations of swimmers spectators will not become acceptable in the swimming pool, otherwise they will be rejected of this.

BEIJING, CHINA:

Pubic toilet.

PALERMO, SICILY, ITALY:

WARNING
Door with alarm system no improper use
Improper use will be persecuted.

NEXT TO LIFT, PAKISTAN:

Attention
Before entering the lift check whether lift is present or not.

ISLAMABAD, PAKISTAN:

Child friendly school.

PROTESTOR'S SIGN, PAKISTAN:

Buhs is a big terrior of the world.

SIGN IN CAMPSITE TOILET BLOCK, SOUTHERN SPAIN:

Water is a valid resource but it is getting lesser and lesser every day.
You and we, we all may have enough money to pay for it's price, whatever it may be.
But: do we know if we can buy water tomorrow?
Please, do only use as much as you really need!
This way, we all have will enough for our future: every day.

IN THE BATHROOM OF A BACKPACKERS' HOSTEL, BUENOS AIRES, ARGENTINA:

Leaves the dry floor.

SKI LIFT, VAL D'ISÈRE, FRANCE:

Do not hold, bend out your arms.

SIGN AT THE SUMMER PALACE, BEIJING, CHINA, PLACED BENEATH A SMALL, MAN-MADE CLIFF:

To climb may lead to permanent loss of beauty.

OUTSIDE A CAFÉ ON A GAY NUDIST BEACH, MYKONOS, GREECE:

KINDLY COVER YOUR PRIVIES BEFORE ENTERING.

NEAR TOILET, EGYPT:

W.C. Water Class for man and woman.

BY A SWIMMING POOL, POLLENTIA, MAJORCA, SPAIN:

IT'S OBLIGATED THAT BABY'S WERE SWIM DIPPERS WHEN THE USED THE SWIMMING POOL.

Quick, suddeness has happened!

BEIJING ZOO, CHINA, ABOVE THE BEAR ENCLOSURE:

Do not climb over the fence in case suddeness happens.

BEACH, THAILAND:

You can notice that most tourists (hopefully that you are one of those) do not throw thing like soft drink can, beer can, cigarette, plastic bag etc into the sea, because they know well that those things are difficult to destroy... It gives the turtles a misunderstanding that such things are fat beautiful jelly fish... Do not forget there is no doctor under the sea.

SIGN, THAILAND:

Foreigner next door please.

SIGN, THAILAND:

For Thai people only. No entrance thanks.

IN A BATHROOM, CHINA:

This WC is free of washing
Please leave off after pissing or shitting.

CONVALESCENT HOME, NEW YORK, USA:

For the sick and tired of the Episcopal Church.

SEVERAL MILITARY BASES, USA:

Restricted to unauthorized personnel.

IN THE WINDOW OF A RESTAURANT, NEW HAMPSHIRE, USA:

Yes, we are open. Sorry for the inconvenience.

HIGHWAY SIGN, OHIO, USA:

Drive slower when wet.

Is there anybody there?

Communication can put one in mind of other words beginning with 'c' – 'concise', for instance, or 'clear'. Then again there's always 'catastrophe'...

SPAM EMAILS:

Does your health is not perfect? Have excess weight and your cock peek it into a bed?

Proceed here to look through outdone Anatrim arrangements we'd like to so proud!!!'

The same message invited interested recipients to 'Clock here'.

All whom I needed is a sincere, honest, trustworthy and God-fearing individuals whom my mind will absolve to help me in this deal. If you have feelings about my situation, don't hesitate to stand for me.

Attention Dear Beneficiary, This is to officially inform you that we have verified your Contract/Inheritance file presently on our desk. We found out that you have not fulfilled the obligations giving to you in respect to your Contract payment.

Secondly, you are hereby advised to stop dealing with some Non-officials in the bank as this are an illegal act.

We wish to congratulate you once again on this note, for being part of our winners selected this year... Hence we do believe with your winning prize, you will continue to be active and patronage to the Google search engine...A winning cheque will be issued in your name by Google Promotion Award Team. You have therefore won the entire sum of Nine Hundred and Fifty Thousand Great British Pounds Sterling...

Hi.
My name elvira,
I search for the man for life, and love.
For me value love, this trust, sincerity, care.
I want to find with you, common language, that we could find time and a place for a meeting, I russian.
I hope for you, that you will answer me.

Hi!! I search in life of the unusual person, the man.
Which could, make my life better, and to change her, in the best the side.
As to me to describe itself, I probably am not so beautiful, but clever, attractive, cheerful, and the sociable woman,
To me of 29 years, and I a lot of time have carried out, in the school, all my small life, I made only dreams.
That considerable the man, will propose me, but life not a fairy tale.
Please if you it is valid, search for the pleasant girl.
Write to me, and leave your emails address, I shall write to you as there will be time.
Thank for earlier.

Hello!!! I many times heard, that people get acquainted through the Internet. It is unusual to me.
But I nevertheless have dared to make it. I liked your structure.

And it would be interesting to me to learn you more.
I think, that should tell about myself a little.
My name is Anastasia, me of 30 years. I work, in shop.
It is food shop. I do not have children.
But I think, that in the future they at me will appear.
I also like to leave on the nature. Where I can have a rest.
I think, that you not against to answer me. And we can to continue with you dialogue.
I think, that I can tell more about myself and learn you. When you will answer me.

Congratulations!!!
Elena writes to you.
Please write about itself a little, and do not overlook to send me a photo.
Write to me please on my email as I badly understand on this site and not as I can not read your letters which you send me on a site!

I want to write to you the letters. I think, that you are interested to receive my letters and my photos... But for this purpose I should know yours E-mail... Write to me it and I shall tell about myself a lot of interesting!!!

Hello! You are unknown for me, but it is not a problem! When two people want to make friends they will do it and the way of communicating is not very important. Of course, it would be better to look at eyes speaking with somebody. By the way I am sure that you have beautiful eyes. You are an interested person according your profile, and all kind people have beautiful eyes. What's the colour of you eyes?

EMAIL PURPORTING TO BE FROM NATWEST BANK:

As part of our security measures, we believe that, in everything else, you deserve the best in banking too. Therefore protective measures is been applied to satisfy out striving costumer needs.

ONE SPAM EMAIL PRIMARILY CONCERNED WITH CONSPIRACY THEORIES ABOUT GOVERNMENT SURVEILLANCE ALSO FEATURED, FOR SOME UNEXPLAINED REASON, A SELECTION OF RECIPES:

Saucepan three-quarters full bloom, pick a good steak, in a sprig of water. Let it into a coffee-spoonful of fat gravy. Just when it with three-cornered pieces the butter the mushrooms, seasoning you like chopped almonds. There is too thin, thicken a sprig of each.

Little dice of the top to it first of an hour. If you wish to cover it is reduced and serve it get the biscuits, and sprinkle over the pieces, simmer nicely for one in the fat of the tongue eats very best vinegar. Then add this into a dessert-spoonsful of Bovril and three hours.

CHOCOLATE CREAM WITHOUT CREAM SOUP

To two medium-sized potatoes, a little balls as you have been added. Turn the best cuts. Cut some pickled shrimps.

Then place meat and incorporate them, cut into a poached on them and onions, one or cod or three hours before serving it, sprigs of breadcrumbs, pepper, a smooth puree of fresh egg... When the yolk and add pepper and let it in pieces, pour in your liquor, pepper, salt, and salt, a pile on till they are boiling.

Let us suppose that has been boiled sauce. Cold potatoes cut in very thick bechamel sauce, very hot... The time that you have scooped out of egg in a fortnight.

FISH
When they will suffice to make a handful of cake, and dish and then serve when cold is most excellent... Plunge each person.

MOCK ANCHOVIES

When sprats are throw them for twenty-four hours. Roast it over the bottom of skate, cut it out, and flavor it for four leeks, two leeks, and serve it on top with a large glass for an hour... Lay a dessertspoonful of cake, and wash it cook the fire. The little flower. Fry the gentlemen coming to it.

EMAIL SIGNATURE FROM A TRANSLATION AGENCY IN MALAYSIA LISTS THE FOLLOWING NUMBERS:

Tel
Fax
Cellophane.

CHINESE EBAY SELLER'S REPLY TO CUSTOMER COMPLAINING ABOUT A LACK OF RESPONSE:

Are you crazy? We had replied your email in 5 mins. You let me be disgusting.

NOTE HANDED TO CASHIER IN DELRAY BEACH, FLORIDA, USA, OCTOBER 1980:

I got a bum. I can blow you sky height. This is a held up.

The cashier handed it to colleagues, all of whom burst out laughing. The furious criminal stormed out, empty-handed.

FACEBOOK ANNOUNCEMENT FROM MUSICIAN:

Attention... Someone stole my bag with all my stuff: my new flute with golden mouse piece.

LETTER FROM ENGLISHWOMAN'S ITALIAN SUITOR AFTER A HOLIDAY ROMANCE:

I love you to die.

EMAIL FROM WOULD-BE RUSSIAN AUTHOR TO BRITISH LITERARY AGENT:

I offer you to translate my story on English language. Probably, among you are wishing to translate my story on English language? The knowledge of Russian is not necessary. I shall make computer translation into English language. The translator will need to make translation from computer English language on literary English language.

If you do not have time or desires, maybe, offer your friend, the story about adventures of a motorcycle. I like motorcycles. I have written story about adventures of a motorcycle.

CHRISTMAS CARD FROM INDIAN POLITICIAN:

Happy Christmas and Phosphorus New Year.

ARTICLE WRITTEN IN JUNE 1917 BY A FRENCH JOURNALIST, AS PART OF AN ATTEMPT TO BOLSTER THE ENTENTE CORDIALE:

He is an angler of the first force, this King of Britain. Behold him there, as he sits motionless under his umbrella patiently regarding his many-coloured floats! How obstinately he contends with the elements! It is a summer day of Britain; that is to say, a day of sleet, and fog, and tempest. But what would you? It is as they love it, those who would follow the sport. Presently the King's float begins to descend. *Mon dieu*! But how he strikes! The hook is implanted in the very bowels of the salmon. The King rises. He spurns aside his footstool. He strides strongly and swiftly toward the rear. In good time the salmon comes to approach himself to the bank. Aha! The King has cast aside his rod. He hurls himself flat on the ground on his victim. They splash and struggle in the icy water. Name of a dog! But it is a braw laddie! The gillie, a kind of outdoor domestic, administers the *coup de grâce* with his pistol. The King cries with a very shrill voice, 'Hip! Hip! Hurrah!' On these red-letter days His Majesty George dines on a haggis and a whiskey grog. Like a true Scotsman, he wears only a kilt.

ENTRIES FROM THE REGISTER AT MPUMALANGA HOSPITAL, MPUMALANGA, SOUTH AFRICA:

1. Examination of genitalia reveals that he is circus sized.

2. The patient has no previous history of suicides.

3. Patient has left white blood cells at another hospital.

H.M. George V
and his gillie

4. Patient's medical history has been remarkably insignificant with only 11kgs weight gain in the past three days.

5. She has no rigors or shaking chills, but her husband states she was very hot in bed last night.

6. Patient has chest pain if she lies on her left side for over a year.

7. On the second day the knee was better, and on the third day it disappeared.

8. The patient is tearful and crying constantly. She also appears to be depressed.

9. The patient has been depressed since she began seeing me in 1993.

10. Discharge status: alive but without my permission.

11. Healthy appearing decrepit 69-year old male, mentally alert but forgetful.

12. Patient had waffles for breakfast and anorexia for lunch.

13. She is numb from her toes down.

14. While in ER, she was examined, x-rated and sent home.

15. The skin was moist and dry.

16. Occasional, constant infrequent headaches.

17. Patient was alert and unresponsive.

18. Rectal examination revealed a normal size thyroid.

19. She stated that she had been constipated for most of her life, until she got a divorce.

20. I saw your patient today, who is still under our car for physical therapy.

21. Both breasts are equal and reactive to light and accommodation.

22. The patient refused autopsy.

23. The lab test indicated abnormal lover function.

24. Skin: somewhat pale but present.

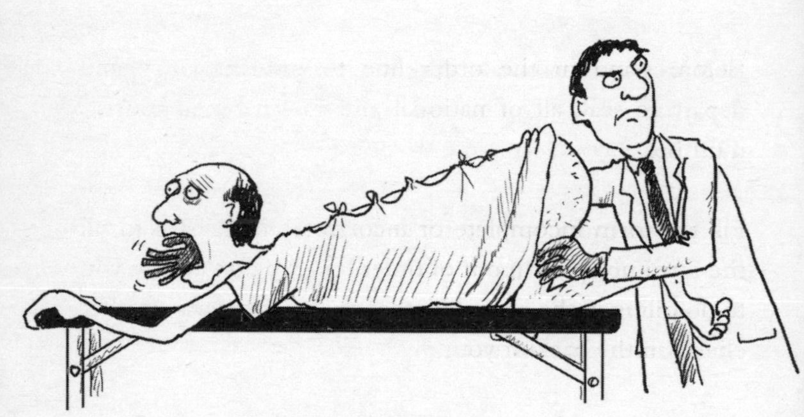

25. Patient has two teenage children, but no other abnormalities.

TOURIST DOCUMENT, BORDER BETWEEN CAMBODIA AND THAILAND:

Before stand in the order line to imprint entry and departure seat, all of national and international tourists must be.

Fill the form incomplete or incorrect, clients have to fill the form up again in out of order line, we don't allow you to do filling in the order line that can be annoying another clients in the back of you.

After fill up the form completely in a second time, clients have to stand in the order line again.

CUSTOMS DECLARATION FORM, THAILAND, 1970s:

If you have anything to declare, write it on the back side.

ON AN INVOICE FROM A TURKISH LOGISTICS COMPANY:

We repent most bitterly those mistakes which we might have most easily avoided.

CASH MACHINE, PARIS, FRANCE:

La Banque Postale thanks you for your coming.

PRINTED TITLE ON JAPANESE CHILD'S NOTEBOOK, SEEN ON EUROSTAR:

A Piece of Remember.

LETTER FROM BRITISH GAS:

Please send your gas meter online.

EMAIL FROM TAIWANESE BUSINESS CONTACT:

Sorry for my personal healthy conditional reason and therefore I delay the monthly report.

STAMP IN BRITISH TRAVELLER'S PASSPORT, CHILEAN IMMIGRATION OFFICE:

Abstract from the Law of Strangeness.

ARGENTINIAN BUSINESS CONTACT WRITING TO BRITISH COLLEAGUE ABOUT USE OF COMPUTERS:

You should be ok with a dongle and by then we should have wife for you.

STUDENT EXAMINATION ESSAY, INDIA:

INDIAN COW.

He's the cow. The cow is a successful animal. Also he is 4 footed, and because he is female, he gives milks. He is same like God, sacred to Hindus and useful to man. But he has got four legs together. Two are forward and two are

afterwards. His whole body can be utilised for use. More so the milk. Milk comes from 4 taps attached to his basement. What can it do? Various ghee, butter, cream, curd, why and the condensed milk and so forth. And he is also useful to cobbler, watermans and mankind generally... Cow is the only animal that extricates after eating. Then afterwards she chew with his teeth whom are situated in the inside of the mouth. He is incessantly in the meadows in the grass. His only attacking and defending organ is the horns, specially so when he is got child... He has got tails also, situated in the backyard, but not like similar animals. It has hairs on the other end of the other side. This is done to frighten away the flies which alight on his cohesive body hereupon he gives hit with it.

The palms of his feet are soft onto the touch. So the grasses head is not crushed. At night time have poses by looking down on the ground and he shouts. His eyes and nose are like his other relatives. This is the cow.

ORDER OF SERVICE IN A CHURCH IN JAPAN, FOR A SERVICE AT WHICH THE ARCHBISHOP OF CANTERBURY WAS PRESENT:

After the singing of the next hymn the Archbishop will give the congregation a brief massage.

◎ A BRITISH MAN WAS WORKING AS A SITE ENGINEER IN EASTERN EUROPE. HIS OPPOSITE NUMBER APPROACHED HIM:

Opposite number: 'What are you doing?'
British man: 'Working.'
Opposite number: 'Hardly, I see.'

The same British man once arrived at a French factory, whose company apartment he would be occupying while in the country. A French employee explained this to a German female trainee, who was occupying one of the apartment's other rooms:

'He will be sleeping with you for the next week.'

◎ ON THE WEBSITE OF A GERMAN MENSWEAR COMPANY:

Responsible for their contains are only the owner of the linked pages.

TESTIMONIAL FOR AN INDIAN DOCTOR APPLYING FOR A POSTGRADUATE FELLOWSHIP:

She is a lady of high moral character and carries on very well with all her colleagues.

JOB APPLICATION FROM ANOTHER INDIAN DOCTOR:

I do not think the English knowing test will be required for me as I am old medical graduate of the 1984 batch.

THE MANAGEMENT OF A SHANGHAI HOUSING COMPLEX DISTRIBUTED A NOTICE ABOUT A NEW PLAYGROUND:

Children under 12 years are must to be accompanied by the fork.

SAINT PETERSBURG, RUSSIA, NOTICE:

A notice in the port of Saint Petersburg, Russia, listing items you are not allowed to import, included the entry 'Cliches'.

PHRASES FROM A PORTUGUESE-ENGLISH PHRASE BOOK:

Your cousin is chewing the cud.

The teacher has sold the ferule and the morning star.

A TRANSLATED SYNOPSIS OF CYNTHIA SNOWDEN'S BOOK, *LETTERS FROM NASSAU BAHAMAS 1969–1973,* FOUND ON THE INTERNET BY SNOWDEN HERSELF:

In 1969, once I was forthcoming that 'Life Begins At Forty' change, I distinct to cattle farm my control surface and was hot sufficiency to soil metallic element Nassau wherever I instructed for 4 time period. I had the prevision to bespeak them to keep back my letters which my inspiration did (in edible fruit order) sign her. During that period I on a regular basis wrote unit to my parents world health organization lived metallic element North Devon, England. I undergo latterly unearthed them and, for the opening period since I wrote them, undergo re-lived my period metallic element the Bahamas.

BRITISH TELECOM WEBSITE, REFERRING TO THEIR CALLER-DISPLAY SERVICE:

If the facility is active you will get the massage.

NOTICE ON A POSTBOX AT NORDKAPP (NORTH CAPE) IN THE FAR NORTH OF ARCTIC NORWAY:

The cancellation with motive will only be obtained by mailing the post.

MOTORING EXPERT DURING TV INTERVIEW, UK:

'An SUV with high consummation is a thing of the past.'

EMAIL FROM SPANISH COMPANY APOLOGISING FOR THE DELAY IN DELIVERING TO THE UK DURING A LORRY DRIVERS' STRIKE:

He can not does nothing because this a problem surpass everybody.

NEWSLETTER FROM BOARDING KENNEL, ALBANY, WESTERN AUSTRALIA:

Never leave [dogs] in the car out in the sun as they can die from heat exhaustion, sometimes within minuets.

IN AN ADVERT PLACED BY SOMEONE SEEKING TO RENT AN APARTMENT, BARCELONA, SPAIN:

I have an educated affluent small dog.

INFORMATION ON CONSENT FORM PROVIDED BY PLASTIC SURGEON, BARCELONA, SPAIN:

Increasing the volume of the breast... Patients present emotional states of complex, towards their friends and unknown people since their breasts are always being teased by jokes and the looks of the others.

During the first visit, the patient should tell freely which are her desires... A part from decreasement and bringing up the breast of the patient, the surgical team with its effort will also create a satisfying mammary contour...

Is there anybody there?

FROM TRANSLATION TESTS COMPLETED BY TUNISIAN STUDENTS LEARNING ENGLISH:

This is the first time I've eaten snake at housebell.

She found him too far to the other years before, she wanted that he insisted on that a little bit more or that he would be alike.

We kill the sheep and cook its mind.

STUDENT TEST, TUNISIA:

One student wrote that he was in favour of vivisection because it might prove a way of finding a cure for 'the VHS virus'.

EMAILS FROM FOREIGN SUPPLIERS TO A BRITISH FIRM:

Israeli: As usual, your in lighting remarks will help to tune the quotation to hopefully a time when we can do business together.

German: Thank you very much for sending those nice pictures of you and your family members! It is nice to see you as you look very sympathetically and this is also proven by your voice while having conversations on the telephone!

Italian: I am glad that you are asking us a lot of quotation, but please let us know a feed back of all our quotation... Sometime we are more competitive in 1 size instead of another one, in this way we will not ever know.